D1220619

Outskirts Press, Inc.
http://www.outskirtspress.com

Paperback ISBN: 978-1-4787-9239-0
Hardback ISBN: 978-1-4787-9303-8

Cover and Interior Illustrations by Oan Somboonlakana. All rights reserved - used with permission.

Outskirts Press and the "OP" logo are trademarks belonging to Outskirts Press, Inc.

PRINTED IN THE UNITED STATES OF AMERICA

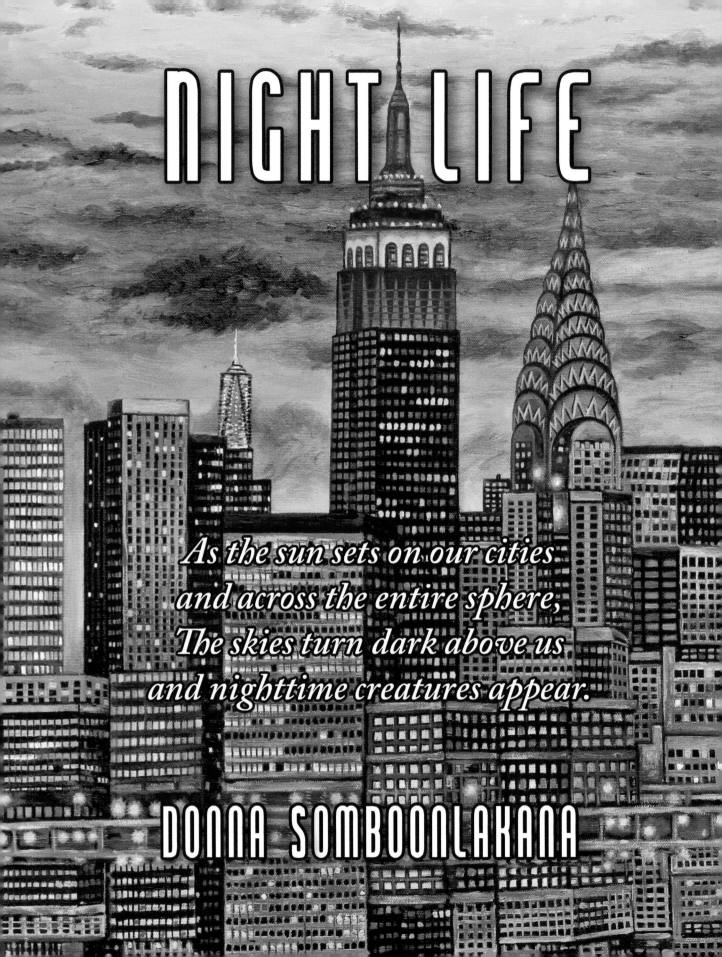

NIGHT LIFE

*As the sun sets on our cities
and across the entire sphere,
The skies turn dark above us
and nighttime creatures appear.*

DONNA SOMBOONLAKANA

Night Life

As the sun sets on our cities and across the entire sphere,

The skies turn dark above us and nighttime creatures appear.

We don't see them very often, but may hear some sounds they make,

Because it's mostly when we're sleeping that they are wide awake.

Some creatures that live in the darkness of night

Have very special ways of living without light.

Different worlds exist between the nighttime and the day;

That's how we share the earth together — in nature's special way.

Bats

In dark places a bat resides;

The only mammal that actually flies.

Because they're unable to lift off the ground,

In order to fly, they hang upside down.

Large bats have wingspans of up to six feet

And bumblebee bats are so tiny and sweet.

Most have the ability to echolocate;

It's a method of seeing that works really great.

They send sonar pulses out into the air

That bounce off near objects then return to their ears.

When these pulses arrive with different timings,

They can then visualize their surroundings.

So, "Blind as a bat"? Au contraire.

Bats fly in the dark and catch bugs in the air!

Raccoons

Raccoons are very clever creatures;

Their human-like hands are valuable features.

They can climb up or down things really great,

As their long hind feet can twist and rotate.

Together, this bunch can make a huge mess;

They tear, gouge, and shred with amazing success.

When roaming around they sniff scents from our trash,

And if they smell food scraps, raccoons have a bash!

So excited to reach a fresh garbage treat,

They'll toss the trash all over the street.

Fitting dark masks on each raccoon face,

Like bandits, they'll take off without a trace.

Huddling together in a favorite old tree,

They protect each other to remain wild and free.

Rats

Rats can live in places that are rather gritty

And are cozy in dark tunnels underground in a city.

They don't live far from their daily food source,

Like uneaten food from restaurants, of course.

When falling from heights of fifty feet to the ground,

They may simply get up and start walking around.

Rats can swim and spend days treading water

And squeeze through small holes the size of a quarter.

They'll enter your home for shelter and food,

Then leave you their droppings and ruin your mood.

Rats gnaw on things like wood, pipes, and brick

To file their front teeth, which grow back so quick.

A rat's front teeth grow five inches per year.

They'll chew on anything; it's a lifetime career!

Owls

Owls are active during the night;

Night vision helps them see in low light.

The owls' senses are very intense,

and a benefit to them at others' expense.

With ears located in two different places—

One high, one low, on the sides of their faces—

An owl can actually pinpoint a sound;

The slightest noise and the prey is found.

These carnivores that only eat meat in their diet,

Will sneak up on prey with feathers so quiet.

After gulping prey whole, as they prefer,

They'll regurgitate pellets of bones and fur.

These stealthy birds with awesome hearing and sight,

Are magnificent hunters during the night.

Rabbits

Rabbits are crepuscular and stay up day or night;

They enjoy early morning hours and evening twilight.

A male is called a "buck" and a female is a "doe;"

Rabbit pairs breed so fast their families always grow!

With long ears equal to the size of its head,

It is no wonder rabbit hearing is so widespread.

Some can jump to heights of three feet in the air

And can leap nine feet when they're out on a tear!

Their eyes have amazing panoramic vision,

All these skills combined help them make fast decisions.

Pet rabbits are quite popular, and if you want one of your own,

Remember that these social animals should not be alone.

If you choose to raise a rabbit, please try a neutered pair,

Because companionship is so important to their welfare.

Coyotes

Long-nosed coyotes with large bushy tails

Are quite vocal with sounds like yelps, howls, and wails.

Parents will huff at their wayward pups

To warn and guide them as they grow up.

These omnivores eat fruit, grasses, and meat

And are not very picky about what they eat.

They indulge in rodents, rabbits, and frogs

and may even eat pets such as small cats and dogs!

It is not wise to feed them or leave food out,

As these "American jackals" will return, no doubt.

People move near canyons and the countryside,

Leaving fewer places for them to reside.

Seen roaming the cities, both small and large,

They'll leave when sensing they're not in charge.

Skunks

The genuine beauty of a black-and-white skunk

Is often ignored because of its funk.

The skunk's fluffy swirled and striped coat

Is easy to recognize when you take note.

When exploring around, they walk fully armed,

Loaded with five rounds if they are alarmed.

A frightened skunk will never fail

To turn, aim, and shoot from under its tail.

Skunks hit their target from ten feet away,

In case you decide to approach one, one day.

Curious animals that are unaware

Quickly learn that skunk oil is too much to bear!

So, be careful when letting your pet out at night;

Confronting a skunk is much more than a fight.

Cockroaches

Cockroaches are incredibly strong

But they rest in dark places all day long.

There are four thousand species of roaches worldwide

And on boats, planes, or trains, they'll take a ride.

They can see in dark places without any light

For the few hours they're active during the night.

Feeling the air move when someone approaches

Is a defensive skill of these sensitive roaches.

These cold-blooded insects can live a week with no head,

Stay a half hour underwater then stroll on ahead.

They can scurry around up to three miles per hour;

Survived nuclear bombs—such a display of power!

These long-legged critters will always creep and crawl,

And it is likely that they will outlive us all.

Opossums

Opossums, or "possums," as most people say,

Are gray-and-white marsupials native to the USA.

The mother nurtures small babies in a pouch;

Growing up, they rest on her as if she were a couch!

Opossums are slow but can climb like champs,

And hang from their tails that grab like clamps.

While strong enough to take a venomous bite,

They'll quickly "play possum" when sensing a fight.

Stressed possums will faint onto the ground;

They can't move at all or make any sound.

Their noses foam with their eyes and mouths ajar,

Their bodies stink; the event is bizarre!

If the possums awaken when they're no longer tense,

Appearing to be dead was indeed a good defense!

Porcupines

It is exciting to see your first porcupine,

The large prickly rodent with its spear-laden spine.

The keratin quills on its head, sides, and tail

Is the same substance found in our hair and nails.

These quills are medicated with an antibiotic

In case it sticks itself when things get chaotic.

Black-and-white quills are an impressive defense;

They'll rattle to warn you when the porcupine is tense.

Every stiff quill is like a razor-sharp pin

And it will charge backward to push them into your skin!

Energetic pets too excited or thrilled

Often end up with a mouth full of quills!

These herbivores enjoy foraging out on their own

And likely won't hurt you if you leave them alone.

Spiders

There are about forty thousand species of spiders.

After spinning a web, they're not the best hiders.

Their silk threads sprawl out from place to place,

And clearly, we see the webs taking up space.

When making their webs they will climb and sink,

Then wait to trap insects for a blood-thirsty drink.

Rocking webs alert them of a brand-new catch,

Then their eight legs run to grab it very fast.

Hungry or not; it is never too soon,

They'll just wrap and save the bugs in a cocoon.

One strand of their silk, though it may seem unreal,

Is five times stronger than the same strand of steel!

While not every spider likes building a web

Every spider can spin a silk thread.

Frogs

Metamorphosis is a change of a great wonder,

Like a tadpole to a frog, from one form to another.

Frogs lay their eggs in water so that the eggs will thrive,

Then the eggs swell up and the tadpoles arrive.

These speedy little tadpoles swim without a care,

Then changes start to happen causing them to be aware.

Their hind legs grow first, and the front legs trail,

The eyes pop out when they lose their tails.

Developing lungs is the final stage,

Taking the first breath, beginning life's new page.

Leaving the water to live on the land,

Croaking unique sounds like a loud natural band.

Passing insects are tempting as frogs stay afloat,

Their sticky tongues will catch and toss them down their throats.

Feral Pigs

America's wild pigs are called Eurasian Boars;

They wandered from their pens after reaching our shores.

Their population grew from a few missing swine

To several million hogs that still breed all the time.

One of the smartest animals seen roaming around,

These pigs became nocturnal to avoid being found.

They forage in the darkness with jaws so very strong,

Cracking nuts and bones till everything is gone.

They cause a lot of damage making sure they get their meals

And can be very noisy with loud grunts and piercing squeals.

We must find a way to control all this pork;

Some say, "Sit at the table with a knife and fork!"

Hedgehogs

Prickly hedgehogs are quite popular pets,

But they're banned in some places and considered pests.

They have spiny coats with fur bellies and faces,

They're friendly, quiet, and adapt to most places.

When searching to eat worms, insects, or snakes,

They toss up the soil and give gardeners headaches!

Digging near hedgerows while searching for prey,

Snorting like hogs, they were named for their ways.

When frightened or sensing an oncoming fight,

They defend themselves by escaping the fright.

They curl into balls lined inside with hair

And extend their outer spines with intent to scare.

Hoping that predators reject their pointy feel

and turn around to go find another meal!

Snakes

Most snakes are harmless, black and small,

And some reproduce without any males at all.

Shedding dead skin a few times each year

Gets rid of the bugs and keeps their skin clear.

About one in four snakes are venomous

With powerful toxins that are dangerous.

They use their tongues to smell, like a nose,

And can strike quite fast, before anyone knows.

These slithering carnivores are unable to chew,

But they can eat large animals; it's amazing to view!

With flexible jaws and mouths open wide,

These reptiles push their meals down inside.

A large meal will make a snake's body bloat;

Astonished, you'll wonder how it fit down its throat!

Fireflies

Some living things can produce their own light;

Bioluminescence is how they brighten the night.

A chemical reaction is the essence

For why fireflies have bioluminescence.

These gentle bugs twinkle over the land

And it's fun to watch one beam on your hand.

Flashing lights help them find a mate

And it's such an easy way to communicate.

Their glow warns predators not to haste,

As lightning bugs have a terrible taste.

Fireflies produce light most efficiently;

The chemical mixture helps release energy.

Their beams of light produce no heat;

Nature's perfection is so hard to beat!

Rooster

Before the daylight is due to arrive,

A rooster's crow sure lets you know you're alive.

He'll begin his crowing early in the morning,

When people are in bed, still sleeping and snoring.

This male chicken has a life that's rather zen;

Only one rooster is needed for a dozen hens!

He struts through the barnyard flapping his wings,

Then when he stops, lifts his head to sing,

"Cock a doodle doo!" to all neighboring friends;

While he is just beginning, you may wish it were the end.

The rooster will keep crowing, loud and strong,

And settle down in darkness; it won't be too long.

The nocturnal creatures described in this book

Are only a few when you begin to look.

There are many more, and I'm sure you'd agree

That most of these creatures we may never see.

So be kind to the creatures that you do get to see

Enjoy them and live life harmoniously.